The Professional Practice Trap

How to Escape the Big Challenges Faced by Service Firm Owners

Shawn Terrell

Terrell Financial, LLC
Windsor Heights, Iowa, USA

Table of Contents

Chapter 1

The Hard Truth

I have some bad news. Your professional practice isn't worth as much as you think it's worth. In fact, it might not be worth anything at all. And, there's little you can do about that.

Might as well get all *that* out of the way. And right away. The service firm owners I interact with prefer it when I am "Straight-Shooter Shawn." So pardon my bluntness out of the chute.

If understanding the value of your service firm (or lack thereof) *doesn't* interest you, then you need not read any further. Then again, that's exactly why I decided to write this book.

I finally reached a breaking point, and decided I had to do something about it.

You see, I've encountered way too many business owners – consultants, dentists, attorneys, etc. - that are unknowingly stumbling or tumbling toward what I call *The Professional Practice Trap,* and it's a tragedy. It's not fair that the business model for service firms forces the owner to retain so much personal risk.

What's The Trap? It's an owner's miscalculation about how to reproduce personal cash flow *without* active work and ownership in their professional practice.

This miscalculation often stems from an over-reliance on the expected future sale price of their professional practice – falsely thinking the proceeds from an eventual sale will solve all future financial wants and needs. But that's far from the only contributing factor to The Trap.

Even owners who are realistic about the enterprise value of their practice are at risk. And the consequences are potentially devastating.

But there's good news - maybe I should mention that, too. It's possible to escape The Trap.

Can you imagine edging closer to retirement and *not* caring how much your practice is worth without you? That's what escaping the Trap feels like. It's being in a position where any net proceeds from a future sale will be "gravy."

This book will give you the freedom to be comfortable in assuming your business is worth absolutely *nothing* someday.

Now, maybe you're already aware that your practice isn't worth much – now or later - without you actively working in it. That puts you ahead of the curve, but it doesn't automatically put you on Easy Street.

There's still plenty of work to be done. The following pages will help either verify or invalidate the plans you've made to this point.

Even if you're decades from exiting your practice, this book contains an enormous amount of information that you'll benefit from learning *now*.

And if this book changes the life of even one owner, the effort will be worth it. My heart is with owners of professional practices, because I'm one too.

If you read this book in its entirety – and that should take less than an hour – you'll learn the following:

- What is the Professional Practice Trap?
- Why do owners fall into it?
- What are the consequences of falling into it?
- How does someone avoid falling into it?
- What's the end result achieved by escaping it?

Fair warning – some of the information I'm about to share might make you squirm. It could disrupt a few closely held beliefs. It might challenge a viewpoint you've cultivated up until now about your practice and how it's intertwined with your personal financial picture.

For those that don't engage, you risk giving up some of the lifestyle that you currently lead. One alternative ending is potentially being forced to compromise on that. You haven't toiled all these years to leave compromise on the table.

If you're a little jarred by what you've just read, mission accomplished. There's too much at stake to bury your head in the sand. So I hope you'll read on. It may very well help you avoid The Trap.

Chapter 2

The Big Contradictions

Our greatest strengths are often our greatest weaknesses. Are you familiar with that concept?

I know, it sounds a little cliché. Yet, I believe it's especially true for owners of professional practices. Like myself. And maybe like you, too.

The best things about you and your professional practice are also the reasons that maintaining that business and your way of life can be challenging.

Not everyone knows this. But that's okay. We're all works in progress.

If you're already "in" business, then you know your formal training didn't provide much of a foundation on how to start and maintain a professional practice.

At the outset, if you fumbled something, it wasn't the end of the world. You probably didn't have much to lose in the beginning anyway.

But now you do. So it's critical you start to familiarize yourself with how to get *out* of business someday. That's true whether you hope to retire next week, or several decades from now.

A little education just might help you avoid The Trap. It's not something you'll likely hear about at the next industry convention.

But before we get there, for context, let's start by discussing a few contradictions about most professional practice owners...

Uncommon Knowledge and Skills

One of your biggest strengths is your unique skillset and knowledge. People seek you and the professional service you provide because of your expertise. You've spent a great deal of time (and probably money, too) on your training and education. You are considered a specialist.

When you combine those characteristics with the courage and vision to hang out your own shingle, the result is a level of income that is uncommon to most others on the planet. You're compensated amply, maybe even handsomely, for your active work in the practice you own.

Now the downside – As a principal in a professional practice, the vast majority of the revenue is a direct result of you working "in the business." As a result, the business might not be worth much without you in it.

That's not to say it's worth nothing without you. It might be worth six or seven figures to the right buyer under the right circumstances.

And it's nothing you've done wrong. It's more of a reflection of the marketplace for professional practices. They don't usually sell for big multiples. And, as we discuss the next example of strength vs. weakness, it will become apparent why that's a big deal.

Uncommon Lifestyle

The uncommon income you earn from your active work and ownership in your professional practice affords you an uncommon lifestyle.

Where you live, what you drive, and how you spend your free time away from the practice are all a reflection of the income generated from your specialized set of skills and knowledge.

That's a good thing, but here's the catch: The comfortable, maybe even luxurious lifestyle you're able to enjoy while actively involved in your practice can be difficult to maintain for an extended period of time once you no longer actively work in or own your professional practice.

And as we alluded to a bit ago, the sale of your professional practice probably won't net some massive amount of money. Again – not chump change - but relative to the amount of money it took to fund your lifestyle while you were active in your business, the sale of your practice won't put you on autopilot forever.

In other words, you could count on *something* from the sale of your professional practice, but don't expect a pot of gold at the end of the rainbow that can satisfy all your financial concerns in perpetuity.

And while many owners assume their personal "overhead" will decrease once they're no longer actively involved in their business, that tends to be the exception more than the rule. Further, given the choice and unlimited free time, why would anyone want to live on *less* money?

So that's a big riddle that needs examination. And guess who gets to figure it out?

Uncommon Independence

The nice thing about being a business owner is you answer to no one. It's open architecture. You have a blank canvass to design and run your business exactly as you see fit.

Want to redesign your office space? Go for it. Want to work three days a week? Give it a shot. How about decreasing your workload by adding more staff? By all means.

Before I go any further, I'm not at all painting the picture that it's been easy to reach your level of profitability. But along with the anxiety and the risk of owning a business comes a level of freedom that money can't buy.

And by now you know I'm going to point out the downside in all of this....

The good news: it's all up to you.

The bad news: it's all up to you.

So as it relates to figuring out a way to maintain the comfortable lifestyle you've gotten accustomed to after you no longer have ownership in your professional practice... it's all up to you.

That can get tricky. If you aren't sure how to navigate it all and make a misstep, you may find yourself in *The Professional Practice Trap.* And you don't get a do-over.

If you're the type of owner that's always looking to learn and grow, then read on.

If you're the type of owner that has attained success with tunnel vision and by blocking outside noise, that's okay too. Now might be a good time to check out. But before you do, please read the first line of this chapter one more time.

Chapter 3

What is the Professional Practice Trap?

The word "trapped" makes me visualize a situation where I have no options. Or at least no good options.

When someone is trapped, any available options will most likely lead to undesired consequences.

Does anyone really want to end up trapped in anything or anywhere (let alone with their practice) *on purpose?* Of course not.

So when people end up trapped, it usually happens unintentionally. Meaning – they didn't understand their present actions would lead to bad results in the future.

And it's the same with The Professional Practice Trap. No owner really wants to end up in it. On at least some level, it's caused by a lack of education... which is why I'm writing a book on the topic.

So with that context, let's examine The Trap a bit further.

What *leads* to the Trap (or where the problem starts) is an inability to generate the cash flow that is required to meet the owner's lifestyle objectives *without* using the professional practice as the origination point of that cash flow.

Framed another way, without revenue from active work and ownership in a professional practice (combined with any value from the sale of it) can an owner continue to produce the level of cash flow required to lead the lifestyle they desire?

If your answer is *anything other than* a resounding "yes," then you may be at risk of getting trapped.

And one big consequence of getting trapped is being forced to make financial compromises. Compromises that, in hindsight, may have been avoidable.

Let's take a deeper look...

The Monthly Nut

Many business owners are familiar with the term "monthly nut," but I'll explain it just in case. The "nut" is the total amount of money the owner must net to cover his or her cost of living in any given month.

More specifically, the nut is the minimum total of salary and profit distributions the owner needs to make his or her personal life "go 'round."

Some people factor it with a worst-case scenario in mind. In that regard, it's the absolute minimum dollar amount an owner needs each month to cover basic essentials like food, clothing, and shelter.

Others factor their number in more realistic terms and include all the amenities they'd like their lifestyle to include – vehicles, vacations, clubs - beyond just the basics.

In other words, when examining what an owner wants their life to look like, how much money does that require on an annual or (more precisely) monthly basis?

Moving Target

Early in the life cycle of a professional practice, it can be challenging for an owner to "hit the nut." That's primarily because any new venture can have unpredictable revenue.

Best case - the compensation hits a level that allows you to keep the lights on and feed your family.

Depending on your specific situation, there's a high probability you couldn't actually pay yourself (or pay yourself what you're worth) in the early months or years of your practice.

If you were able to pay yourself, chances are it was because you bought existing cash flow from your practice by borrowing money.

Either way, given the unpredictable revenue in the early stages of a practice, the monthly nut is usually lower.

Even if there is good cash flow and revenue early on, any rational owner will want to make sure they establish a repeatable pattern of profitability before taking on more financial obligation.

Memory Lane

To fully grasp this concept, think back to your time in college, graduate school, or the like. What did your personal residence look like then? What about your vehicle or transportation options? Could you afford much in the way of recreational activities or vacations during that time?

I'll go out on limb and guess your education and training years were not a time of great extravagance. Most survive that period on what can be earned with any part-time work and can be borrowed via student loan programs.

And since everything that's borrowed needs to be paid back, and there's a cost (interest) in whatever amount is borrowed, most borrow just what they need to meet basic needs.

Fast forward to the early days of your professional practice (if you're beyond that point). Maybe you traded in three roommates for one spouse. A bike for a car. A spring break road trip in a borrowed minivan for a direct flight to a quieter destination.

Now... look at your life today. Has the size and value of your house improved since you first decided to go into business for yourself? What about everything else? Maybe you've added a few stamps on your passport. Do you now hope to fund significant life events for your children, like college or weddings?

You see, everyone builds a life and a lifestyle around the expectation of the income they will generate. For the professional practice owner, "life" is built around the specific expectations of salary and profit distributions from the business. And that expectation changes – usually by increasing significantly – over time.

Unconscious Upsizing

As professional practices generate more revenue and pay down debt, the profit margin grows. Life and lifestyle have a way of keeping up with that growth. It happens so incrementally that it's easy to miss unless you look backward and recognize how much it's changed for the better with the passage of time.

Gradually, maybe even unconsciously, you've "up-sized" over time... or it's reasonable to expect that you will. The "nut" will most likely continue to grow. That's not necessarily bad news. Most people hope their lifestyle improves as they progress in their career and life.

But here's the catch... Do you ever want your worst-case scenario to be worse than it is now? As owners move up the lifestyle ladder, do any ever want to go back down? Would you want an involuntary downsizing to be on the table? Most people hope to avoid that.

That's tricky, because at some point in the future, the amount of money needed to satisfy the lifestyle nut won't come from you actively working, and it won't come from profit distributions as a result of practice ownership.

It will have to originate from alternate sources. And, as mentioned earlier, any proceeds from the sale of your practice will help with that, but probably won't carry the day.

And so, in order to avoid The Professional Practice Trap, at some point in the future you'll have to engineer a systematic way to generate the cash flow required to meet lifestyle objectives (the nut) without your practice as the source.

The consequences of failing to optimize that process can put a reduction or downsizing of lifestyle on the table.

It will take some level of advanced planning to have a shot at an optimal outcome. Because there will absolutely come a time when you exit the marketplace and from your practice. Hopefully, that exit occurs voluntarily. But there is a 100% chance that it occurs. It's inevitable.

Shrinking Nut

Now, I do want to acknowledge that the cost of lifestyle could be lower in the future.

Some owners may be inclined to cover the cost of private high school, college, and the wedding of multiple children. Assuming the kids all successfully "fly from the nest," the cost of children is (mostly) eliminated.

Maybe your "forever" home eventually gets paid off too. The nut could be lower in the future.

The question I always ask is: "Do you actually *want* your cost of lifestyle to be lower in the future?" Or maybe more critically: Do you want to be caught flat-footed and with limited options if the cost of your lifestyle *doesn't* decrease as expected? Does that sound like being trapped?

If that's something you'd like to avoid, it's critical to educate yourself on why many owners inadvertently fall into The Trap. That's where we're headed next.

Interested in that? Read on.

Chapter 4

How Does an Owner Get Trapped?

I hope what I'm about to write won't cause anyone to confuse me with Confucius…

With that disclaimer: We don't know what we don't know.

Remember earlier when I posited that no owner would intentionally end up trapped?

Now that you (hopefully) understand The Trap, we'll dive into three of the most common reasons owners fall into it. And as we make that transition, it starts with the notion that we don't know what we don't know.

Wearing Two Hats

Owners of professional practices often have two jobs. You are probably both the Owner *and* the Operator.

As the operator in your professional practice, you are the person with the training, skills, knowledge and expertise. You are responsible for delivering that to the marketplace – the customers, clients, and patients – and your business receives revenue as result of what you deliver.

You may have a strong team around you, but chances are, your active work in the business is what drives the majority of the gross revenue generated by your practice.

That's a good thing. That's what you were educated, trained, and born to do.

The thing is, that's not your only job. You also own the business. And the education and training you received to be a business owner is probably a fraction of what you received to become a specialist in the actual work that generates revenue.

So, it's not at all uncommon for owners, through no fault of their own, to be unaware that they might be trending toward a long-term problem.

The owners that are able to recognize this potential blind spot and can humbly seek to educate themselves have a much better chance of dodging The Trap.

No General Contractor

A cousin to the previous problem is the lack of coordination between the business advisors the owner does rely on.

Between investments, the qualified plan, health insurance, life insurance, disability insurance, property and casualty insurance, malpractice insurance, bookkeeping, tax preparation, and legal documents for both business and personal affairs, an owner might have relationships with a dozen "advisors."

And chances are, while these advisors all (hopefully) have expertise in their specific areas, they're all sub-contractors, so to speak. They may lack the knowledge and expertise to help the owner understand how all the various pieces fit together.

What tends to be missing is an advisor that has the expertise to play a role like a general contractor does in the construction industry. That can go a long way in an owner understanding their situation from a high-level, holistic point of view.

If you've ever built or remodeled a house or your practice space, then you know the poor coordination that often manifests among all the sub-contractors. That type of disorganization is often found when looking under the hood of a professional practice.

Additionally, just like construction, there's a hierarchy of action that should be followed. It would be unwise to start the flooring or drywalling without first securing the roof. And yet, figuratively, that's what sometimes inadvertently happens with practice owners.

A general contractor can make all the difference. The result is improved business-related decision making.

Overconfident in DIY Abilities

Perhaps the most dangerous are professional practice owners that are overly confident they can figure all these issues out on their own. They believe in the DIY (doing it yourself) approach.

Remember when I said earlier some of this content will make people squirm? I was referring to this type of owner in particular... They think they know, but they don't know.

What's ironic is that owners of professional practices encounter this type of client or patient in their own practice on a regular basis. The internet has made everyone an expert in everything.

When someone *actually is* an expert, it's a test of strength for that expert to clench their teeth, smile, and nod along as the "expert" postulates theories to the *actual* expert.

Imagine the physician that's traversed medical school, residency, and fellowship training only to be cross-examined by the patient that spent five minutes on webmd.com? I digress.

I'm probably teetering on the edge of bluntness, but the point I'm trying to make is that expertise in one discipline doesn't often translate to expertise in an entirely different discipline.

It can be tough for owners to recognize this potential blind spot, and it's complicated by the fact that business owners are often professional problem solvers. They're used to figuring everything out on their own.

**As an aside, I don't believe most people actually *want* to figure out how to do things on their own – but I'll save that digression for another book. **

Winging It

This is probably the most common reason owners stumble. Most owners are "winging it" in trying to figure out the best way to generate the cash flow life requires beyond ownership in their practice.

In the philosophical context we've used in this chapter, winging it can best be described as owners knowing they don't know… but doing the best they can to figure it out. Again, the problem solver trait can sometimes be a weakness here as well.

Winging it might look like:

- Understanding the need to save profits for later, but not knowing how much to set aside.
- Understanding the need to invest money, but being unsure on the most efficient way to do it.
- Understanding the objective of reducing taxes in the present year, but not

understanding the lifetime effect of tax deferment.

- Understanding the need for insurance, paying a lot for it, but unintentionally leaving gaping holes in some areas.

In short, owners that wing it are doing the best they can. On some level, consciously or not, they tend to recognize that they probably have some exposures in their world. But their optimistic nature makes them believe if they get most of the parts and pieces right, it should work out okay.

The Time Crunch

What stops the owner that recognizes potential flaws from taking more powerful action? Time. There's a reason time is the most precious commodity for all of us.

Show me a successful professional practice owner, and I'll show you someone who spends so much time working "in" the business that they have little capacity to work "on" the business.

And when you break it down, it's easy to see why. Think about all the responsibilities that soak time and attention from the professional practice owner:

- Doing the work, or performing the skills and providing the expertise that generates the majority of revenue. The work might pay

well, but that doesn't mean it's not intensive and mentally draining.
- Business development. Many practice owners not only do most of the work that directly produces revenue, it's also likely they have to spend time generating new client opportunities.
- Managing employees. Having a team can be a great resource. However, it can take some time to not only get the right people on board, but also in the right roles or "seats."
- Family. Most of the professional practice owners I know are incredibly committed to their family. It's not all about work.
- Recreation. Another commonality – owners tend to work hard-play hard. That might mean frequent travel and fine dining. Sometimes it's hunting, fishing, or golfing. What good is freedom and flexibility with money and time if you can't enjoy it?

So when you examine all these different factors, you can understand how an owner could accidentally find themselves trapped. And that's not a good place to be, unless you're okay with the consequences of being trapped.

What are the consequences and what does that look like? We're headed there next.

Chapter 5

What Are the Consequences of The Trap?

Have you ever had a client or patient that didn't take your advice or follow your treatment plan?

You can stop laughing now. Of course you have.

You're not alone. I've experienced plenty of the same in my work. And when a client fails to take the action I recommend, it's sometimes because they just don't care about the potential consequences – no matter how severe - of *not taking* action.

Early in my career, that used to drive me crazy. But eventually I accepted that there's a certain percentage of people that will never act in spite of all evidence to the contrary. Maybe you can relate.

From my perspective, the potential consequences of an owner falling into The Trap are pretty severe. But I recognize not everyone will see it that way.

With that disclaimer, what are the consequences?

At a really high-level, the potential consequences of The Trap are being forced to compromise in some fashion.

In a practical sense, what might that look like?

Working Longer than Desired

Most professional practice owners know they've only got so much gas in the tank. There will always be a few outliers that desire to work until they keel over. But for everyone else, there's a finite number of years where the skills, knowledge and desire form a Venn Diagram.

Imagine a scenario where you can't work as efficiently and effectively as you used to, feeling burned out, and yet knowing that for financial reasons, you must "soldier on" actively working in your professional practice? That's what The Trap looks like.

On the other hand, maybe you're still in top form as you enter the home stretch of your career. Maybe keeping up on the latest trends, technology, and hammering out CE's isn't a burden, but the pull of enjoying more time outside the practice has increased.

Whether it's the grandkids, the desire to travel, or the interest in spending more time on your hobbies, your interest in your work and ownership may wane as you enter the twilight of your career.

What if your financial position didn't allow you to do anything about that "pull?" That's what the trap looks like… Being forced to stay longer than you'd like.

Riskier Sale Terms

Earlier, we briefly touched on the premise that for most professional practice owners, the net proceeds from the sale of the business cannot solely be relied up to generate the cash flow needed for retirement. Some practices might not have any value beyond liquidation.

For the practices that do have transferrable value and can be sold upon your exit, it's worth noting the way the sale is structured can put owners at risk of being trapped.

Ideally, the sale and transfer of ownership in the practice will occur simultaneously with the financial reliance on it coming to an end. But things don't always work out that way.

Some deals are structured in a way that the selling owner will receive future payments from the buying owner for a period of time after relinquishing control of the business. This type of deal is sometimes referred to as an "earn-out," and it might be worth avoiding if possible.

If you agree to an earn-out sale, then you're still financially dependent on the practice, even though you no longer have control over it. It adds a significant and unnecessary level of risk to your exit from the practice.

What happens if the new owner isn't as good as running the business as you were? What if the new owner takes on an unnecessary amount of new overhead? What if your clients and patients don't like the new owner as much as they liked you?

All of those factors can have an effect on the profit margin of the practice... The same profit margin from which you are supposed to be systematically paid for the transfer of your ownership interest. What if that margin shrinks significantly?

What happens if some other set of circumstances lead to diminished revenue for the practice? A reduction in margin doesn't necessarily indicate poor management or bad behavior from the new owner. The new owner will have the same external risks that you had as an owner.

In a tug-of-war between rent, payroll, and your earn-out, who gets paid first? Maybe the better question is: who gets paid last?

Being forced to accept an earn-out solely because it represents (theoretically) the highest total purchase price is bad position to be in. If the highest bidder can't secure institutional lending, you should ask yourself why.

Sure, if the new owner defaults on the terms of the sale, you might be able to reclaim ownership. But what will be left to take back? Does it sound good potentially being tethered to that for months or years?

Waiting every month for your check that's allegedly "in the mail" is what The Trap looks like. Avoiding an earn-out helps you avoid the trap.

Reduction in Lifestyle

Another version of the trap is being forced to compromise on your lifestyle long after you've cleanly separated from your professional practice.

We'll dive deeper into this in the following chapters, but at a high-level: The sum of assets created and held outside the practice, combined with any net proceeds from the sale of it will be used to generate the cash flow that is required or desired for the rest of the owner's days.

Whatever that total number ends up being, it needs to be able to fund all lifestyle objectives for the rest of your and/or your family's days. At least that's the objective.

And people have a way of underestimating that objective. Is an owner who exits his or her professional practice after several decades an expert at generating cash flow from active work and ownership in a business? Probably yes.

Conversely, that same owner has to next figure out a way to generate (realistically) a similar level of cash flow for several more decades from assets uncorrelated to that business. What are the chances they fail to account for everything it takes to successfully accomplish the latter?

Moreover, the owner only gets one shot to get that right. Not getting it right may result in lower cash flow being produced.

If lower than expected cash flow is produced from assets in retirement, that shortfall has to be accounted for somehow. And one of the ways it could be accounted for would be for the owner to spend less money.

In practicality, that means reducing the money spent on lifestyle in retirement: lodging, experiences, toys, meals, or helping out children or grandchildren.

That month-long European cruise you've been talking about for years? How about a week in Branson instead?!

I'm kidding, and there's nothing wrong with Branson. I'm just trying to make a point.

It takes expert planning to identify and properly account for all the threats that could lead to a compromise in lifestyle. And there's no do-over.

Returning to Work

Similarly, if a reduction in lifestyle isn't preferred or even possible, then another option to make up the short fall and increase revenue would be returning to active work.

This is assuming to return to the workplace is physically or mentally possible. Remember, the sale and exit from the practice occurred for a reason.

Additionally, there may be licensing and continuing education considerations. If the exit from the practice occurred many years prior, this alone will make it difficult to return to the marketplace.

And if we're being honest, ego is a consideration as well. If someone owned their own professional practice for decades, how well will they tolerate being (more or less) forced to work for someone else?

Similarly, for the prideful types, how would that look to family and friends in the social circle? That's no big deal so some folks, but others would do just about anything to avoid that outcome.

Sound like being trapped? Want to learn more about how to avoid any of those scenarios? Read on.

Chapter 6

Regeneration: Reaching the Tipping Point

If you're still reading, I'm going to make a few assumptions about your mindset: You recognize you could be at risk for falling into The Trap, you understand the consequences of falling into The Trap, and you'd like to avoid those consequences if at all possible.

So that begs the question, what actions can be taken to avoid The Trap?

At the highest of levels, The Trap is avoided if the cash flow required to fund the life you desire can be generated in perpetuity from sources *other than* your active work and ownership of your professional practice.

Accomplishing that involves a few steps, and we're going to reverse engineer those steps. That means we're going to start by discussing the desired end-result first: *Regeneration* of cash flow.

The objective is to replace the cash flow produced from active work in your business from different sources – or regenerate cash flow from somewhere else.

In order to do that, you'll need to arrive at the retirement age window – the preferred age range when you'd like to have the option of exiting your practice - with assets outside of the practice.

Those assets become the new origination point for the cash flow or income you require for retirement.

One approach with that: Taking a portion of the total assets from outside the business and siphoning any earnings and/or the principal from those assets on a monthly for annual basis to meet lifestyle objectives in retirement.

Another approach: Exchanging a portion of the total assets from outside the business for guaranteed lifetime payments from an insurance company on a monthly or annual basis to meet lifestyle objectives in retirement.

Whatever approach or method is employed, the ultimate objective is to regenerate cash flow from assets outside the business and use that regenerated cash flow to replace the income that was created from working in and owning your professional practice.

That probably doesn't happen by happenstance. It most likely will involve a fair amount of planning and discipline. In the absence of being able to do that effectively, lifestyle compromises may have to be made.

For the time being, we're going to snap our figurative fingers and assume you have reached the point where you believe you can effectively generate the desired cash flow from assets outside your practice. That's a big assumption, but this approach is helpful in framing the ultimate objective.

This is a key point, so let me reiterate: We're starting with the end in mind. Once we've established what the ultimate objective looks like – again, producing desired cash flow from someplace other than your practice – we'll reverse engineer how to get to the Regeneration stage – the desired destination.

The Tipping Point

When you reach the point that the amount of income required to satisfy your lifestyle objectives can be generated from assets built and held *outside* of your practice, you've reached what I call *The Tipping Point.*

Reaching The Tipping Point equates to a belief that you are no longer financially dependent on active work and ownership of your practice.

At this point, you are able to produce enough cash flow from outside assets to do whatever it is you would like to do for the rest of your life without continuing to actively work in and own your practice.

How much money do you need on a monthly (or your preferred frequency) basis to do everything you want to do when you're no longer working in your practice? That number is your Tipping Point. That number is your objective.

I realize that term *Tipping Point* is neither original nor catchy, but I hope it is at least understandable and easy to remember.

Because the Tipping Point is probably one of the most (if not *the* most) important financial objectives for any professional practice owner.

It's the point at which you have, financially-speaking, the ability to retire or go do something else. Another way of describing this point is that the owner becomes financially-free (another unoriginal, yet easy to understand term).

Remember when we discussed how, when building and growing a practice, your lifestyle is built around the expectation of the profit that can be derived from your active work and ownership?

Similarly, your lifestyle in retirement will depend on the cash flow that can be generated from assets outside of your practice. When you've verified that you can generate the amount required, you've reached *The Tipping Point.*

In the pages ahead, we'll dive further into the actions required to both achieve and maintain tipping point cash flow. As I said, that will take some planning and discipline. But for now, let's address a more couple key points about hitting that big threshold...

The Tipping Point Varies

The tipping point is different for everyone. That's because the lifestyle objectives are different for everyone. People have different plans, goals, and desires for their post-practice lives.

An ideal retirement for some might be traveling the world, fine dining, owning big houses and vehicles, and the desire to substantially support children and grandchildren.

Others might seek to downsize their house and car, take a few road trips, and spent as much time as possible roasting marshmallows and hotdogs around the fire pit.

There's no judgement if you're more or less inclined to pursue either scenario – to each their own.

The point is, the tipping point for some might be the ability to generate $50,000 per year in after-tax cash flow. For others, the target might be $500,000. That's big difference. So there's a big spectrum in terms of the amount of planning that could be required.

The Numbers *Not* to Focus On

It's worth noting that, as you've thought about retirement, you may have done so with a different number in mind. You're not alone. The marketing departments of financial institutions everywhere have done a masterful job of reinforcing this concept.

The "number" for our context here is the total sum of all income-producing assets needed to replace the income being produced by active work and ownership in your professional practice.

As an example, someone might add up their 401(k), IRA, taxable investment, and savings account values to reach their "number."

While your total amount of assets is definitely relevant, what matters above all else is the amount of *cash flow* that can be generated from those assets. And the math on that calculation isn't always as simple as some may portray it.

You'll reach the Tipping Point when the amount of cash flow that's desired for your retirement lifestyle can confidently and continuously be generated off your total assets – no matter the sum of those assets.

Net Worth is another number that is over-emphasized as it relates to someone's retirement picture. It's not *irrelevant,* but it's not the best number to focus on either.

That's because net worth accounts for at least some assets that are either illiquid or are unlikely to have much capability of producing cash flow or income.

Take your primary residence, for example. The equity in your home could easily account for a half million dollars or more of your net worth. But is that equity likely to produce cash flow? Sure, fads like reverse mortgages come and go, but do you really want to go down that rabbit hole to fund retirement if you can avoid it?

Where I live in Iowa, farming operations are another good example of how net worth can be misrepresentative. A common refrain from farmers is that they are "worth a lot on paper, but cash poor."

That's another way of saying that the value of the farmland they own doesn't always have a direct correlation to the cash flow – or in some years, even profit – that will be produced.

Some types of businesses or operations generate a low amount of cash flow relative to their valuation as an entity.

And when examining this concept from the reverse perspective, we arrive back at one of the major premises of this book: Some businesses are worth a relatively *low* amount of money when valuated (or on paper) as compared to the high profit they produce. Sound like your professional practice?

Owners spend decades expertly managing cash flow while active in their practices. The focus should remain on your (tipping point) cash flow as you engineer your financial life in retirement.

Hold Off on the *For Sale* Sign

The other thing to note is that hitting the tipping point doesn't mean you have to stop actively working and sell your practice. It just means that you don't *have* to keep working because you need the money.

There are other reasons besides the financial component that people work. Active work and continued ownership in a professional practice beyond the tipping point is common.

If you've worked in your practice for decades, it's probably at least in part because you get some purpose or satisfaction out of that work, and that doesn't automatically stop once you reach The Tipping Point.

In fact, some people will never retire. There are examples of people whose health took a dramatic turn for the worse not long after they stopped going to the office every day.

Those that find purpose in their work might notice a correlation to that and their overall health. So for those that want to keep their foot on the pedal as long as they have the ability to do so, more power to you.

So in that sense, reaching The Tipping Point may not be the ultimate goal. Having options is the goal. Choice is the goal.

Once an owner reaches The Tipping Point, they have the choice to design the rest of their life as they see fit.

Chapter 7

No Backflow: Maintaining Tipping Point Cash Flow

As we just outlined, one of the primary objectives in avoiding The Trap is to reach a cash flow Tipping Point. It's the ability to regenerate cash flow from assets outside the practice, rather from ownership and active work in it. What else is important to know about The Tipping Point?

It's not enough to reach The Tipping Point for the first year of retirement. The objective is to maintain the level of cash flow required for lifestyle objectives each year in retirement. Every year in retirement. For the rest of your life.

I'm no plumber, but having recently fixed my sump pump, there needs to be a backflow valve related to The Tipping Point. Once someone reached that threshold, there need to be measures in place to make sure the cash flow never goes backward or below The Tipping Point again.

To that end, a few different elements can put that objective at risk and need to be accounted for. What or where are the areas of the financial picture that, if not fully understood, can have negative effects on cash flow in retirement? The following are the top four items that need to be examined:

Longevity

I've lost track of how many clients have expressed some version of the following: "I can't see myself living past 85 or so..." Really?

Often, that assumption stems from how long the client's parents or grandparents lived. On some level, it's also a reflection about how the client thinks about their overall health and habits.

And the client may absolutely be right. They might not need cash flow to live beyond the age of 85. Heck, they might not survive more than one year of retirement. But is it appropriate to actually plan based on that assumption?

Without going too deep down this rabbit hole, it's reasonable to expect health care and medicine to continually evolve and improve. Thus, people have better odds to live longer in the future, all things being equal.

And by underestimating how long you'll live (and how long you'll need money) you open the door for the fear of running out of money to enter the picture in your later retirement years.

Notice the distinction there... I believe it may be rare for someone to completely run out of money in retirement. Rather, what's more likely is that assets could start trending or drifting downward at an accelerated rate, leading a retiree into a scarcity mindset.

It's similar to how at my house, we never run out of milk. We just start to ration it if the jug is getting low and there's no trip to the store on the horizon. Once there's a second, full gallon in the fridge, we return to an abundant milk mindset.

It's a stupid example, but I hope it underscores how the fear of running out is much more common than *actually* running out of money. No one wants to be a financial burden to their children or siblings, and by accounting for longevity - how long you may need to generate tipping point cash flow - that risk is mitigated or avoided.

It's not ideal to fear running out of money before you run out of life.

Inflation

I'm not interested in some deep analysis about the Consumer Price Index here. But it's important to at least acknowledge the effect of inflation.

As we just alluded to, you might live 30 years or longer beyond the sale of your professional practice. And while it's easy to *not* notice inflation from day to day or year to year, if you look *back* 30 years, you'll probably agree that the things you buy today cost more than in 1990.

So is it fair to expect them to cost more 30 years into the future, in 2050? While everyone's inflation rate is different because everyone's lifestyle is different, you're probably not done buying "stuff" just because you exit your practice.

For example, you'll probably need to replace several cars, appliances, and phones in your retirement years. Each of those new things will probably cost more than the previous version of it.

Healthcare and long-term care might be the most volatile and unpredictable of big potential expenses in the future. Those alone could significantly impact cash flow in retirement. So the rising cost of it, along with everything else, needs to be accounted for as well.

Market Volatility

It's reasonable to expect that you'll invest in some form of equities in building toward tipping point cash flow. Put another way, you'll have some money "in the market"

If that's the case, then you probably have some sense that there are few guarantees with money invested in the market.

As you accumulate money for retirement, you'll probably experienced periods where the market performs both well and poorly.

Are you fully aware how market volatility might affect your ability to generate cash flow when withdrawing money in retirement?

The role sequence of returns plays during the distribution phase of retirement is one area that there tends to be a lack of education.

When investors are withdrawing money from investment accounts to generate retirement cash flow, the timing or the sequence of the rates of return they receive on their money over time can have an impact on their overall account values – thus, how long the money may last.

Even though it's a fairly technical, this is important, so let's use an example:

Take two hypothetical owners considering an exit their respective practices in the next several years – let's call them Jill and Jane.

Let's assume a few constants: Both Jill and Jane own the exact same investment account and will continue to do so throughout retirement. Thus, the performance of the investments – good or bad – will be exactly the same for both from present until the end of the road... and let's say both Jill and Jane will live exactly 30 more years.

Other constants: Both Jill and Jane plan to withdrawal the exact same (flat) amount of money on Day 1 of their respective retirements to cover the annual cash flow needed for retirement lifestyle. Both plan to repeat the same process on the anniversary of their retirement start dates each and every year in retirement.

Now, let's mix in one variable: The actual start date of retirement for each. Let's say Jill decides to retire on January 1st, 2025, and Jane's retirement will begin on the same day in 2030... a five- year difference.

In that scenario, with the start year of withdrawals being the only variance, the total account values will be different for Jill and Jane when looking into a fixed time period in the future.

In other words, even though both Jill and Jane are invested the same way and taking the same distribution amount with the same frequency, the overall account balances will be different for each when looking 5, 10, 15 years into each of their respective retirements.

That's because, even if both receive the same average rates of return, the order or sequence in which those returns occur during a period of distribution will affect the overall account value.

That's important because it introduces chance or luck into the equation. Either Jill or Jane could get lucky with their retirement date and end up with a higher account balance than they started with –

despite the distributions – several years into retirement.

However, if either gets unlucky with the performance of the market in retirement, any decline in the overall account value for one or both could be further exacerbated by distributions to generate retirement cash flow.

Can you predict the best year to retire ahead of time? Is it acceptable for you to do everything right for decades, and then get totally unlucky by retiring at the wrong time?

If you plan to primarily use investable assets to generate cash flow in retirement, how critical is accounting for market volatility and sequence of returns risk?

Taxes

If you're like many professional practice owners I know, you've created a qualified plan – such as a 401(k) - as part of your practice. And there's a good chance you're leveraging that plan to the maximum of IRS limits, or expect to do so in the future.

You're doing this partly to save for retirement and partly to defer taxes until retirement. The latter is based on the expectation you'll be in a lower tax bracket in retirement. And thus, the hope is, you'll pay less overall taxes in your lifetime by deferring the income taxes in your working years until your retirement years.

So as you plan for ways to regenerate cash flow in retirement, if you plan to use qualified plan assets to generate some level of income, the taxes that will be due need to be accounted for in the planning.

What if you're in a lower tax bracket in retirement, but the percentage of tax due for that bracket is actually higher that the percentage that was due while you were working and deferring?

Also, if you've built assets outside the business in a non-qualified environment – say in a taxable investment account – then there will be some level of tax liability that needs accounted for on those assets as well.

If you continue to hold certain types of taxable assets in retirement with the hope of continued growth, any growth will lead to additional taxation at some point – depending on what that growth is realized.

These examples bring up the topic of tax diversification. It may be advantageous to arrive at retirement with outside business assets that will be taxed in different ways when income is distributed from them.

You Don't Get a "Do-Over"

It's important to education yourself and get all of these considerations out on the table, because you only get one chance to get it right when it comes to planning for retirement cash flow. There's no do-over.

Not accounting for any of the four items just mentioned can bring compromise back into the equation. Either you have to compromise on the lifestyle you planned to live in retirement. Or you compromise with how you planned to spend your time in retirement because you're forced to return to active work to make up the cash-flow gap. Neither is a desirable option.

So before an owner switches the origination point of their cash flow from active work and practice ownership to assets outside of the business, they need to be darn sure the cash flow from assets can carry the day.

It's somewhat analogous to a child being born. At birth, the origination point of an infant's oxygen supply switches from the umbilical cord to their own lungs. When my son was born, that was the big moment of truth. I was literally holding my breath waiting for him to cry, and thus, breath on his own (he did!).

In a different way, that's how tipping point cash flow needs to be engineered. The owner needs to know it's going to work before he or she sells their practice and gives up that lifeline. The owner only gets one shot to get it right.

Chapter 8

Extraction: Full Realization of your Practice Value

Let's pretend for a moment that you, the professional practice owner, are able to cease active involvement in your business on the timeline you desire.

Let's also pretend that you are able to do that with the cash flow that is desired (as covered in the last few chapters) to meet your lifestyle objectives.

For that to occur, for the ultimate objective to be achieved, what action would have been taken or what would have occurred while you were still actively working in your practice? That's where we're headed next.

Reverse Engineering

As it relates to someday switching the origination point of your cash flow from active work to assets outside the practice, we've just laid out the end result first in the last two chapters...

We've defined tipping point cash flow as the objective and discussed the threats to maintaining that cash flow for as long as retirement lasts. Now, we're going to reverse engineer how to get to that desired end result.

For the ultimate objective to be achieved, what action needs to occur from today until your retirement age window to achieve predictable, sustainable tipping point cash flow?

As we covered earlier, a big part of The Trap is an overreliance (or any reliance) on the net sale proceeds a professional practice. While an eventual sale could lead to a chunk of money, it's unlikely to be a big enough lump sum by itself to generate appropriate cash flow in retirement.

Best case, converting your ownership interest to cash and then back into cash flow will be a slice of the pie. Which means you will need to enter the retirement age window with other assets… assets outside or uncorrelated to the practice.

This reality can actually be viewed as a positive, with a little different framing. What your professional practice may lack in transferrable or enterprise value in a sale upon exit, it may make up for with a (hopefully) significant profit margin along the way.

Now, there can be some variance in the profit margin between different professional practices, so I hesitate to be too specific with margin percentages. But you know that number in your head. It's higher than many other different types of businesses.

Theoretically, the bigger the profit margin during the life of your practice, the less you might expect in the way of proceeds upon your sale of it.

On the other hand, businesses in different industries might command much larger sale prices but have the tradeoff of low margin while the owner remains active.

Framed that way, the positive is that professional practice owners don't have to wait until their retirement party to realize the full value of their business.

Part of The Trap is, some owners don't know or fully understand this concept, so they may miss the opportunity to fully realize the value of their practice.

To quote Jimmy Fallon's character in *Almost Famous* (my favorite movie): "You gotta take what you can, when you can, while you can, and you gotta do it *now.*"

Extracting Value

How do you, the owner, arrive at retirement with outside assets significant enough to cash flow the retirement lifestyle that is desired? By systematically extracting value from the practice throughout the lifecycle of your ownership.

Without some massive payday at the destination, the value of the practice needs to be transferred to you *during* the journey, or along the way.

It's in this sense that a prudent professional practice owner might spend decades, little by little, exiting his or her practice.

A chunk of the profits from the active work and ownership of your practice need to be carved out and separated from business on either a monthly, quarterly, or annual basis.

It's with this approach that the owner has the best chance of entering the retirement age window with an accumulated amount of outside assets that can be used to properly regenerate the cash flow previously created by active work and ownership in the practice.

For this to occur, the value needs to be expertly extracted "along the way," or during the journey of ownership.

How Much Should Be Extracted?

At the risk of being slippery, it depends.

It depends what you want retirement to look like from a lifestyle perspective.

It depends on if you plan to remain active in the business until you're age 50, or until you're 70. The longer the potential retirement horizon, the more initial capital you'll need to meet your cash flow objectives.

It depends what stage you are in of practice ownership. If you're in the early years of ownership, you have more time on your hands to extract value. If you'd like to exit and retire in the next 5-10 years, you might have some catching up to do.

So with that context, let's try to wade into this topic at least ankle-deep: An extraction rate of 20% of gross salary and profit distributions is considered a good rule of thumb. So if you're paying yourself a salary of $150,000 per year and taking an additional $350,000 of profit distributions ($500,000 total), extracting and diverting $100,000 per year to assets outside the business is a good starting point.

Again, if you start extracting early on and expect to live a modest lifestyle in retirement, maybe you can save less.

If student and practice loans prevented you from really socking away much money for the first 10-15 years of your practice, then maybe that extraction or saving percentage should be higher.

There will need to be some modeling done for each owner with extraction rates and the correlation to retirement cash flow.

Where should extracted value be stored?

Short answer – anywhere that it can be used to generate cash flow later – or in retirement after you've exited your practice.

As I mentioned earlier, many practices choose to setup a 401(k), profit sharing, or other qualified plans. This may allow the owner to make contributions as both the employee and match some of those contributions as the owner.

For practices with fewer employees, SEP IRA's might be a way to accomplish a similar objective for a lower cost and less administrative red tape.

Traditional or Roth IRA's are also an option. However, depending on income, the availability or the deductibility of those options can be affected.

Non-qualified taxability investments don't pose as many restrictions, and those are an option too.

Risk tolerance factors in too… in that regard, cash value life insurance could be another place to divert profits. Bank CD's are another low-risk option… though CD's tend to be more attractive in a high-interest rate environment.

Last but not least, real estate or another business entity could be worth exploring too. Perhaps value extracted from your professional practice today could be used to buy those types of assets with the expectation that they generate cash flow down the road.

What are the other considerations?

Remember a few chapters back when I mentioned the idea of "winging it?" It's the term I've coined for owners that do the best they to make smart financial decisions, but don't have the time and energy to vet or ground the actions that they're taking.

"Winging it" is most present during the Extraction Phase, as efficiency and drive lead to increased profitability, but also distraction. That can lead to several issues, such as:

- A "junk drawer" of financial products. The end result might be products that don't always fit together in the most holistic way. Without a general contractor – or if the owner is the general contractor by default – it's doubtful all the pieces will get put together in a coordinated, efficient way.

- Not exercising self-discipline with lifestyle. As your practice continues to be more profitable, you'll be able to afford nicer things. The big question is, *should* you afford those things?

  This is a good problem to have, but spending more on lifestyle today (houses, vehicles, vacations) introduces the risk of *not* extracting or saving enough for tomorrow – retirement.

When someone wants to borrow money to buy something, the lender always examines the total amount of the loan in comparison to the value of the asset being purchased. This is known as the loan to value ratio.

You might apply that same scrutiny to the amount being extracted to generate tipping flow cash flow for "tomorrow," in comparison to the amount of total practice profit being spent on lifestyle today.

Using the 20% saving or extraction objective mentioned earlier, that would make 80% an appropriate lifestyle to income ratio. There's a fine line between living for the today vs. saving for tomorrow.

- Overreliance on rate of return. "Under-saving," or not extracting an appropriate amount of value can force owners into an overreliance on the rate of return they receive on the amount they do save.

You should expect some rate of return on your money. And it's important this expectation is in line with historical rates of return in the vehicle in which the money is being stored.

The rate of savings – or the percentage of overall income that is saved – can actually be a bigger factor than rate of return received on what is extracted.

- Taking unnecessary risk. Similar to the previous example, I sometimes encounter owners that have misperceptions about how much risk they actually need to take with money extracted from their practice.

  As such, these owners put money in places that could generally be categorized as "high risk- high reward." That might turn out to be a good thing, but it's problematic when owners think this is how they *need* to invest.

- Not understanding tax implications. How and where practice value is extracted and diverted will go a long way in determining how much tax will be due while money is being accumulated, and when it's distributed as cash flow in retirement.

  Some accounts are tax deferred until distribution, some generate taxes during accumulation and distribution, and some may be fully-taxed at present but tax-free when distributed if specific rules are followed. Understanding the different tax implications will shape the total amount of tax the owner pays during their lifetime.

Over-Engineering

It's less common, but worth mentioning too that a small subset of owners actually *over-engineer* their tipping point cash flow planning. That is, they account for so many factors and become so gun-shy of the unknown that they end up working in and owning their practice way longer than is necessary.

As I mentioned earlier, it's perfectly fine to stay involved in your practice well into the proverbial retirement years if you *want to*. It's problematic if an owner stays way longer because of a false belief that they *need to*.

In practical terms, that often takes the shape of an owner continuing to extract and accumulate assets outside the business in a much greater degree than is required to generate their tipping point cash flow.

While the owner will absolutely need to make sure they don't sell to soon or without accounting for the four big risks, they can also stay too long.

In that regard, one cash flow design methodology that may be employed is to generate the tipping point cash flow that is desired using the *least* amount of assets as possible. That might sound odd or counterintuitive at first blush, so let me provide a high-level example:

Let's say the owner's retirement tipping point cash flow objective was $300,000 per year, and the owner assumed he or she would need $7.5 million in assets outside the business to safely generate that cash flow throughout retirement.

However, if education and planning make it possible to generate that same cash flow ($300,000) from $6 million dollars without taking any more risk, then the owner may have the option of exiting their practice sooner. In that scenario, they'd need to extract $1.5 million *less* value from the practice in order reach cash flow tipping point.

It's like the person that wants "washboard" abs, exercises two hours every day, and yet eats indiscriminately.

Another path to the same, great abs (not me, for sure) might be a better diet with half the exercise. Similarly, we're looking for the most efficient path when designing the way to generate tipping point cash flow.

With proper planning, what the owner gets back is time. And if there's one finite commodity, it's time.

What Else?

In conclusion, in the last few chapters we've examined the objective of regenerating cash flow from sources other than your professional practice. We've examined both the actions required and the landmines to avoid in order to generate tipping point cash flow.

However, the discussions to this point have focused on exiting your practice voluntarily. What if you didn't leave your practice on your terms? What might cause an *involuntary* cessation in the cash flow you generate from active work?

That's one of the final pieces to understand in avoiding The Trap, and that's what's next.

Chapter 9

Protection: Guarding Against an Involuntary Exit

Throughout this book, we've talked about you exiting your professional practice from the perspective that you'll do it largely on your terms. When you're ready.

Once you've extracted and accumulated the assets that will allow you to achieve your cash flow tipping point, and once you no longer derive the same purpose from the active work and ownership, you can leave.

That might be an oversimplification, but all and all, the idea is that the choice is yours and you'll make these decisions voluntarily.

But what if you are involuntarily forced to leave your practice? Should that be accounted for as well?

Should the rest of you and your family's life, financially-speaking at least, have to look any different than it was supposed to look because of something that happened beyond your control?

Without you generating revenue from active work in the practice, there probably isn't much revenue. Without revenue, there are no salary and profit distributions.

Without salary and profit distributions, would your lifestyle be affected between today and your retirement age window?

And without salary and profit distributions, would it be difficult to extract value and build assets outside of the business to generate tipping flow cash flow for retirement?

The reasons owners are able to build successful professional practices are among the same reasons that an involuntary exit from that practice can get overlooked or not fully accounted for: Optimistic, well-adjusted people don't spend a lot of time thinking about all the things that could go wrong.

And some of the topics we're about to touch on have a low probability of occurring to you. It's much more likely that you will exit your practice on your terms.

But there's an uneven correlation between probability and consequences. And thus, it's prudent to examine the big things that could cause an involuntary exit.

Death

When an owner of a professional practice dies, the revenue that was being generated from the particular knowledge or skill provided by the owner stops, both at present and in the future. The lifetime earnings of the owner are frozen forever.

If an owner dies early in their career, how might that affect the lifestyle the owner's family is able to lead without him or her? Would it have to change, and if so, does that matter?

If an owner dies five years before their planned voluntary exit – and all the revenue that was expected to be generated over the next five years is not realized – how might that affect the retirement lifestyle of their spouse? Would anything have to change, and again, does that matter?

What happens to the practice when the owner dies? Who becomes the de facto owner? Who becomes the de facto operator? Are operating and buy-sell agreements in place and consistent with objectives?

What happens to employees of the practice? What about customers, clients, and patients?

This is not some indirect way of saying "you might need more life insurance." It's merely nudging you into some more thought and analysis than perhaps has occurred previously.

Illness or Injury

The reality is, it wouldn't necessarily take a significant, catastrophic situation to dramatically impact your financial future.

An eye or back injury, for example, might be uncomfortable and inconvenient for a consultant, but not cause a huge disruption in their ability to practice their expertise and generate revenue. For a dentist? It could be a different story.

Those details aside, a disability, illness, or injury has similar financial consequences to death in many ways. It leads to a sudden reduction of gross revenue.

On the other hand, an illness or injury is different than death in that it doesn't always lead to a 100% elimination of revenue. Sometimes an illness or injury causes only a reduction in revenue as the professional practice owner can still work some of the time or do some of the things they were able to do before… just not all of them.

Also, unlike death an illness or injury isn't always a permanent cessation of revenue. It's entirely possible that you could eventually recover and return to full capacity.

I would stop short of a blanket statement that an illness or injury is any less of the threat than death. And that's because I think it's much more likely that an illness or injury *increases* the cost of living.

Think about it… If an illness or injury is severe enough to keep an owner from working and generating same level of revenue as they were prior to its occurrence, is it less likely or more likely that it costs more to live?

And if there is an increase in the cost of living and a decrease in the revenue that is actively generated, how does that affect an owner's ability to continue at the appropriate extraction or savings rate for retirement?

Should your financial life have to look any different because of an accident or because you get sick?

Lawsuit

Besides death, illness, and injury, there's a few other areas that can unintentionally (usually) hamstring an owner from meeting future tipping point cash flow objectives.

A lawsuit could throw a wrench in your future financial picture. There are usually two variations of this – professional and personal – and either can have an effect on both your income and your assets.

A claim of professional negligence of malpractice might put a professional license at risk. If you are required to have a license to receive compensation for the skills you provide within your practice, that's a pretty big problem.

Even if you're not required to have a professional license or designation, a claim of wrongdoing can impact your professional reputation – that also could have an impact on revenue.

On the personal side, lawsuits can originate with an accusation of fault for an event that occurred with some type of property that you own – whether that's a residence, vehicle, watercraft, or something else.

A legal claim made against you can impact the assets you've accumulated or the future income you produce. And that might have a negative affect your ability to someday produce – or continue to produce – the level of cash flow needed for lifestyle objectives.

Decades of hard work and prudent planning could be jeopardized by an accident or a momentary lapse in judgement by someone in your family unit. Understanding liability risk is critical in avoiding The Trap.

Disruption in the Marketplace

Finally, it's worth acknowledging that you need to account for the notion that you can't account for everything. Follow that?

This is my way of saying this chapter is not an exhaustive list of everything that could cause an involuntary disruption or elimination of the income your produce from your practice. It's just a few of the big pieces.

The possibility that your practice could – through no fault of your own – be disrupted by some external force in the marketplace can never fully be eliminated.

Could a change in technology at some point in the future influence the revenue you can generate with your specific skills and knowledge?

What about a legislative or governmental change?

My industry – financial services – has been impacted tremendously by both government regulation and technology over the last 20 years.

Partly because of that, I believe the perception of financial service professionals has also changed dramatically over the last several decades, and it's fair to expect that to continue in the future.

Whatever the industry you specialize in, maybe you can relate.

And it's worth noting that I'm writing this book in the midst of the COVID-19 pandemic. You'll have a hard time finding a professional practice owner that could have foreseen that disruption on the horizon.

Planning for the unexpected can be enormously beneficial when unforeseen circumstances force us to ride the storm out or pivot in a different direction.

Chances are your exit from your practice will be voluntary – on your terms and timeline. But involuntary disruptions and exits must be accounted for too… the potential consequences are just too severe.

Chapter 10

This Book is Worthless...

Remember a few chapters back when I asked, tongue-in-cheek, if you've ever had a client or patient that *didn't* accept your professional advice?

You made a recommendation, and your experience and knowledge left zero doubt in your mind that it was appropriate, and that action was necessary.

Yet for some reason - procrastination, hubris, frugality, fear – whatever – the client failed to act.

You are now in danger of becoming the equivalent of that client.

If you've made it this far – the final chapter of this book - you recognize the risk of The Trap. Doing nothing with the information makes this book worthless. There's a good chance you're exposed somehow, somewhere.

If your professional practice is profitable – meaning you're paying yourself what you're worth *and* taking ownership distributions - then it's time to examine your specific circumstances with more scrutiny.

You will always be busy. And yeah, you may have all the time in the world. And yet, you don't.

Remember in the first chapter when I said my clients prefer me to be "Straight-Shooter Shawn?"

Well, it's time to spend a little time working on your practice instead of always working in it. It's time to check for holes and maybe plug a few leaks.

You haven't worked this hard for this long for it not to turn out how the way you'd like it to turn out. It's time to get buttoned up.

Predictability and Confidence

When you take the next step of examining *your* risk of being trapped, the end result is more predictability with your financial future.

Now, predictability doesn't always have a positive connotation – like when my wife tells me I'm *so predictable.*

But at a really high level, I think that's what people want most from their money – some level of predictability.

When I ask my clients what they want from their money, common responses include: stability, confidence, and freedom.

All three of those things are possible with predictability. Not *predictable,* there's a distinction. More *predictability* than currently exists.

After all, people build a lifestyle around the expectation of the cash flow they will generate. It would stand to reason that predictability around that would be a good thing.

People want to know what to expect. When you know what to expect, you're less anxious about the future. When you're less anxious about the future, you have more peace of mind.

Imagine the confidence you'll feel knowing that if something beyond your control happened tomorrow, your family could continue living the exact same financial life that they are today.

Imagine being confident that the amount of money being extracted from your practice is appropriate for the tipping point cash flow you want to achieve later.

Imagine being in the twilight of your career and not haggling over the valuation for your practice or the terms of the sale.

Imagine a retirement where you go weeks or months without being concerned with the exact balances of your investment accounts. Who wants to log on every day from the beach or lake house?

Imagine having the ability to make a financial impact for the people, institutions, or causes you're most passionate about.

That's what's possible.

Avoiding Worse-Case Scenarios

When you put in the time, energy, and resources to protect, extract, and regenerate the lifetime value created from your work within your professional practice, you significantly increase your odds of avoiding these undesirable outcomes:

- Working longer (more years) than you would like: If you don't properly extract value from your practice during your working years, you'll be forced to stay active in it until you're able to build assets outside of the business to achieve tipping point cash flow.
- Accepting an earn-out deal that leaves your financial future at risk: If you fail to achieve tipping point cash flow before you're mentally or physically unable to continue actively working, you'll have to rely on the sale of your practice – perhaps with unfavorable terms.
- Compromising on the lifestyle you and your family desire and deserve: If you fail to reach and maintain tipping point cash flow, then you may have to cut living expenses to meet whatever cash flow is being produced.
- Returning to the workforce: If you're unable to achieve or maintain tipping point cash flow, and lifestyle compromises are not

possible, then the last option is to return to active work to meet the cash flow required.

Fully realizing the lifetime value of your professional practice doesn't happen overnight, and it sure doesn't happen without your involvement. You will probably have to devote some time and resources to the cause.

But it sure beats the alternative... *The Professional Practice Trap.*

Next Steps

I hope this book has sparked some new thinking and new insights for you. Whenever you're ready, here are two more ways we can help:

1. **Subscribe to our podcast – *Dentists, Puns & Money.*** Navigate to dentistexit.com and click "Podcast." Follow the prompts to subscribe to our email newsletter to be notified when new episodes are released. Also, you may subscribe on any of your favorite podcast apps.

2. **Work with Dentist Exit Planning directly.** Uncover the unique risks associated with your practice and learn action steps to avoid The Trap. If you're a dentist, to find out if we're a fit, visit dentistexit.com and schedule a Discovery Meeting.

About the Author

Shawn Terrell is the founder and CEO of Dentist Exit Planning, an independent Registered Investment Advisor firm providing financial planning for dentists across the United States.

He began his career in the financial services industry in 2011.

For more information, visit dentistexit.com